FRITZ KÜHN

Decorative Work
in Wrought Iron
and other Metals

GEORGE G. HARRAP & CO. LTD
LONDON

Translated by
GILLIAN BRETT

Copyright by Verlag Ernst Wasmuth Tübingen
First published in Great Britain 1967
by George G. Harrap & Co. Ltd, 182 High Holborn, London, W.C.I
English translation: © George G. Harrap & Co. Ltd 1967
Copyright. All rights reserved
Printed and bound by Ensslin-Druck Reutlingen
Printed in Germany

"Nowadays if we are building a new house or refurnishing a flat or taking trouble over anything at all that is supposed to be of relatively lasting value, we find that it is a remarkably difficult business; we guess and grope and nothing seems exactly what we want; we know and like almost everything: the very old as well as the very new, the thick as well as the thin etc. and we change our minds a great deal." These words of Heinrich Tessenow clearly express our uncertainty when choosing an object that we want to buy and can also be applied to its manufacture. Why is this so? Why don't we clarify things? Craft — applied arts — arts and crafts — industrial art — manufacture — industrial design: this questionable vocabulary shows how questionable our concepts have become today. Therefore we have to choose for our requirements things that will not give rise to misunderstandings.

Who has made the maker and the buyer uncertain about recognizing what is right and good? Today we can see the roots of this uncertainty in the industrial revolution, which made it possible for us to mass-produce machine-made articles for the first time. These new machine-made products, which at that time still had no style of their own, were ornamented at first with traditional decorations. These factory-made goods were usually supposed to be imitations of old craftsman-made products. At that time people failed to offer these articles, that had been produced by new methods, as machine-made and to value them as such. We have long since come to realize that both are important and that both are indispensable: that which is mass-produced by machine and that which is unique, created by the craftsman's hand. The one may not — indeed will not — oust the other. Industry has a great part to play in our cultural life, because it alone can satisfy society's enormous demand for, amongst other things, durable consumer goods that are necessary for life today. One could say that everyone comes into close contact with these products, because they have to use them daily. From this fact arises the exceptional responsibility laid upon industry in the design of its models. It must constantly strive to produce good and above all functional designs that can be beautiful, indeed very beautiful, even though they are without decoration; because a good design is already decoration in itself. The craftsman, on the other hand, must create things with mind, heart and hand which industry is not able to make by mass-production; although a machine-produced article of good design can be of more value than a badly executed, insignificant, hand-made one.

Today there are really no longer any definite dividing lines between hand and machine-made articles. Products that are of pleasing design and functional can just as well be made on a machine as by hand, providing man has mastered the machine and made it his tool. It is not the machine in itself that makes the work less good, but our inability to use the machine in the right way. It is wrong to hammer a machine-pressed dish after it is finished. Hammer blows are only beautiful if they are necessary for the shaping. Let us take as an example the candlestick that is illustrated on page 56. It is not forged, that is not shaped with a hammer, but turned on the lathe. Here the lathe, that is the machine, was the tool. On looking at it we think of cylinders, pistons and connecting rods: machine elements. Now it would be nonsensical to hammer this candlestick. It would lose its precise clean-cut lines by it and the final result would still not be a piece of forged work. It would be just as absurd to put the dish that is illustrated on page 13 on the lathe and turn it; because this dish, as the drawing shows, really was fashioned from a lump of glowing iron — naturally with the hammer and without a mould. As it was made in this way it is understandable that the dish is uneven in places. But these uneven parts, just like the visible hammer blows, make it more effective. One knows by the very surface of the dish and the turned candlestick the process and the method which were employed to produce them. I have described this in such detail on purpose, because unfortunately one still sees wrought iron objects in arts and crafts shops, department stores and even at exhibitions, that are supposed to dazzle us by their "beautiful" hammer blows and that are bought on this account as craftsman-made wrought iron work. If one looks at these objects more closely one realizes that often they merely consist of pieces of pre-hammered strap iron bent while cold, the hammering having played no part in the shaping. The individual pieces are then held together by oxyacetylene or electric welding. Such objects are worthless as products of industry, are harmful to craft, even more to arts and crafts and deceive the buyer, who unfortunately does not usually know about these things.

As a craftsman it is not my place to deal with industrial design, nor is that the purpose of this book. What is important is that we creative artist-craftsmen should not be opponents of industrial progress, that we recognize machine production of durable consumer goods and no longer regard the machine as our enemy. From this acceptance we must find the right path which we can follow, not without concern for the future and aware of our mission. Often stones are thrown across this path. On the one hand we are called "romantics". But on the other hand, if we venture a little too far beyond the traditional frontiers of the craftsman, people say reproachfully: "Don't be untrue to your craft, stick to your hammer". Craft is often said to make a cult of outmoded things. In reality, however, the situation is quite different. Craft has, as everyone knows, a great past and consequently a tradition to which it is bound, but where it must not stop. The tradition which craft observes is living and renews itself constantly through the conflict with the demands of the present. Tradition is a stimulus to craft and not a more or less guaranteed pension that craftsmen of today receive as their inheritance from craftsmen of yesterday. Tradition means increased responsibility and duty. Craft can be proud of its past, but must nevertheless be constantly concerned with its present and its future.

To the new generation of craftsmen — whose numbers for all that are few enough — we must point out the importance of the trade and show them the way for future tasks. We shall only preserve our craft in the face of industry, if those employed in it are creative, placing authenticity before appearance and earnestly striving for the best. Anyone who feels that this is his vocation should set to work with both hands and learn to love his craft, so that in this way the beauty of each individual piece which he creates will never cease to give him joy. To craft fall the great and responsible tasks of not only teaching these young people mastery of the material and the methods of working it by practical individual work, but also of developing their sense of design. Then later on, those who feel attracted to technology can decide to go into industry and help to see that its products are manufactured in a good artistic design. Let us in this way preserve the beginning, the start, the craft — indeed the creative craft.

The articles illustrated in this book — with the obvious exception of the few historical ones — all originated in my workshop. Frankly, railings and trellis-work are the best assignments for a wrought iron craftsman. This does not mean at all that one may treat the implements and small things as subsidiary. There are naturally differences of design. When designing a railing or trellis my starting point is always its architectural context and above all its task of protecting, supporting, dividing and affording a view through. With implements and small objects other principles guide me in the design. For the most part they are three-dimensional structures, genuine sculptures, which one can move about and put in different places. Therefore a candlestick, a table lamp etc. must be stable; equally in the case of a knob on a piece of furniture, a door handle, or the handle of a fire-side shovel, one must be able to take hold of it. I mean one really must be able to take hold of these things and, indeed, in such a way that we enjoy having them in our hands while we use them. The usefulness of implements increases their value. But we also fashion things that cannot be judged by their usefulness alone and yet have a function in their relationship to their surroundings and to the human being. They create an atmosphere, which is the expression of a personality or a community. Objects and implements fashioned in this way have a formative influence on our lives and contribute towards making our existence richer and more beautiful.

Anyone who looks critically at the examples of my work in this book will find that they are very varied. It was only at the request of the publisher that I decided to publish some of the implements and other incidental little things that I have made, in varied sequence, from the vessel to the little "bringer of joy" (bird, page 148) that stands at my studio window. I did not select these articles according to any strict criteria. It is simply that for me they are like life itself: gay and serious, difficult and easy, simple and ornate, sometimes shining brightly, sometimes of a dull unassuming shade, often purely functional, often an end in itself, the result of a spontaneous enjoyment and serious playfulness. The functions which have to be fulfilled — in part determined by the client — are manifold. The latter usually has something particular in mind when ordering a piece of work and frequently has certain preconceived ideas about how it should look. The amount of money that can be spent on such an order also plays a considerable part in the making of it. One frequently has to explore, indeed project oneself into, the mind and imagination of the person who has given the order. A monument for a grave is to be forged for someone who has lost his closest companion in life. It will be a modest memorial in the cemetery. He would like to see all his love for this person, indeed the whole being of the dead person, reflected as far as possible in the work. Another time a joyful occasion is the reason for an order. Two people have got married and good friends of theirs want to present them with a candlestick for the wedding. It is to be a symbol of the bond between them, a constant companion on their joint path through life. The a r b o r   v i t a e, the tree of life, was the symbol used here (page 42). A grate for a simple farm-house room with solid furniture was ordered (page 127); a gay wall decoration for a hall or staircase in a country house (pages 84 and 85); another time it was making a lighting appliance that was imposing enough not to look out of place in an old palace (page 111). So it goes on. From the many requests and orders something new, something different, always arises. Clients came laden with lists of requests, which I was supposed to incorporate. Furthermore there are the so-called "nice" orders, the prizes and presentations. An example: the staff of a firm had collected money to give the manager an impressive and expensive present on the occasion of his jubilee (page 88). It had to "look good", as they said. The following were to be incorporated in the piece: naturally his name, the trade he had learnt (he had trained as a smith, that was why it was to be a piece of decorative wrought ironwork), the town where he was born, the town in which he was then working, the workshop which he bad built up and was running, the year of the jubilee. In addition I was supposed to express his love of Nature. In this enumeration I have already sorted the requests and left some out — there were far more. Leaving out is not always easy because in this one has an opponent — the client. So a battle ensues, an often hopeless struggle to make him realize that art also consists of "leaving out". It is vital that now and again one has time to experiment — an order for oneself as it were. This is how the dish with the "velvet skin" came into being, someone else called it "granite" (page 26). What secret does it contain? It has not got a particularly striking shape and yet sensitive, thinking people like it. I had planned a special surprise for my wife's birthday: to give her one flower and not to present her with a bouquet as I usually do. One flower; it was to be a red rose with leaves on the stem. But how should I do it? Walk up to a woman holding one flower in my hand? No, as a man, I did not want to do that. So I considered how I could enhance the rose in all its delicate beauty. I had to place it on some contrasting material. For contrast intensifies the nature of things and the stronger the contrast the more we are aware of this. I placed the rose on an old steel plate. I was startled by the clash between roughness and delicacy. Now of course I could not take a rough steel plate; I did not want the flower to fall off at the slightest movement or gust of wind. So I shaped the material into a large hollow hand, in which the flower would feel safe. The weight and size of the dish were determined by the fact that I had to use both hands to carry it without compressing my chest. So carrying the dish forced me into a good posture and by its weight it also determined my step. Now the surface. The bare iron, beautiful though it was, relieved by the visible hammer blows caused by the shaping, still seemed too harsh for a woman. I had the dish covered with pure gold. I was horrified when I saw it again. To me it looked garish and gaudy. Without a moment's hesitation I rubbed the gold down so that it remained only in the smallest depressions. In this way the dish regained its steel character. All the pores of the material became visible.

The little monogram in the middle was done on so small a scale that it needed to be sought and discovered, and was only intended for my wife. So an implement came into being, serving a purpose, fashioned according to a person's needs with the additional quality of giving the bearer a good posture. Is this the secret of the dish?

"Form is a great deal in art, but not everything. The most beautiful forms of Antiquity were inspired by a spirit, a great thought, which makes the form into a form and reveals itself in it as if it were its body. Take this soul away and the form is a mask!" (Herder). We must not be guided by striving for effect and trying to make an impression when fashioning things, but we must endeavour to make them in such a way that the implements grow closer to our hearts the longer we have them around us. This is as true of a simple present as of an imposing presentation gift. The little candlesticks on pages 32 and 33 want no more and no less than to quietly contribute to the atmosphere by their flickering candle light at a party and to provide the smokers with a light. Even altar candlesticks do not have to be regarded as holy. They have a job to do, a simple quiet purpose to serve, to provide light. Something that holds, collects, protects and communicates: that is what a vessel is. The tensions in the bowl of a dish, the pleasant bell-like ring when it is struck and the unfathomable life in the metal and in the natural colouring — is not this harmony often meaning enough? Such an implement can be a source of natural enjoyment and become a constant companion on our path through life.

Vessel, forged from one piece of sheet steel. The effect of the
vessel is achieved solely by its shape. Transition from the circular
base to the square rim with rounded corners.
Diameter 6.3″.

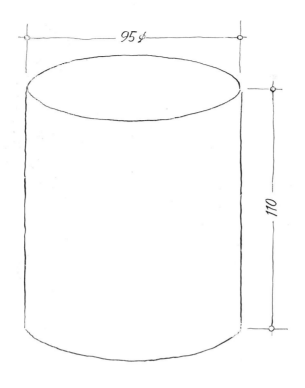

95 ∅

110

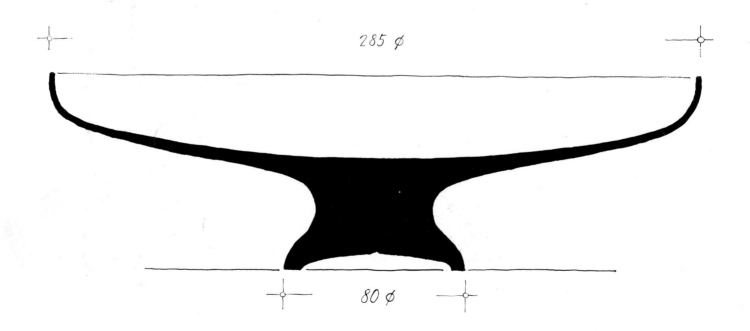

285 ∅

80 ∅

Dish forged from one piece of round-sectioned steel, see drawing on the previous page.

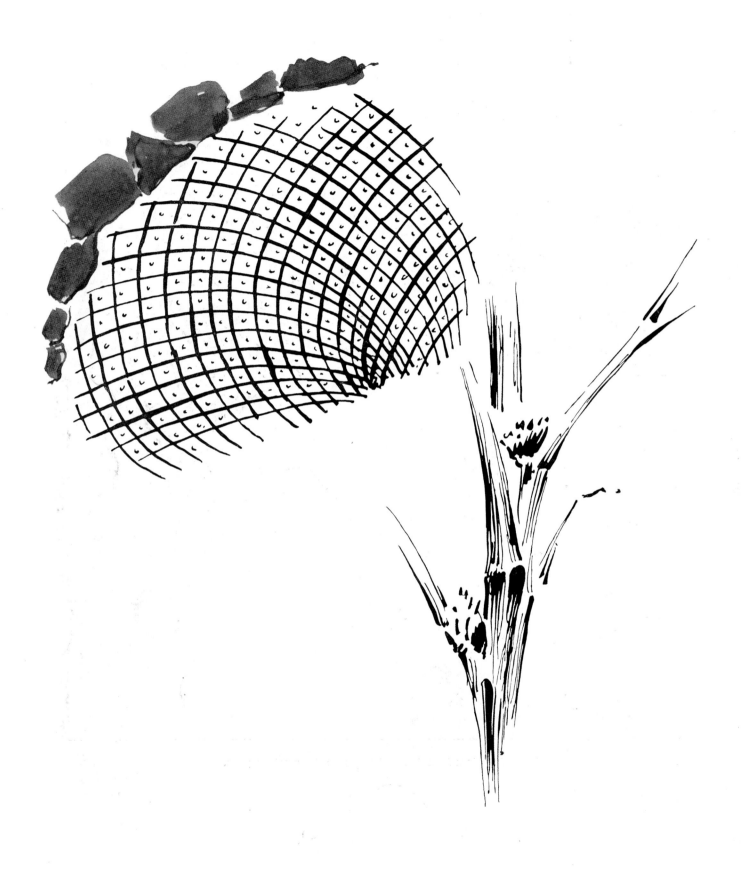

"Sunflower" dish forged from 0.118″ thick sheet steel. Diameter 13.39″
Left-hand page: study of the sunflower from nature.

Dish of 0.236″ thick sheet steel, rim hammered, decoration cherry foliage, chiselled and grooved. Diameter 16.5″. Surface finish: natural colour of the steel after forging preserved by waxing.
Right-hand page: detail drawing and cross section of the dish.

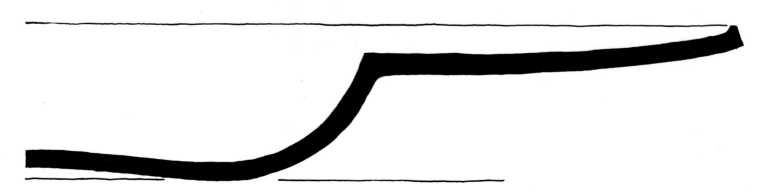

Deep dish of 0.315″ thick sheet steel. Diameter 17″. Rim hammered and grooved. The rosette is worked by the same technique. The grooves of the rim and rosette are gilded.

Dish with ornate decoration. The natural shape of the ear of corn is so greatly stylized that it has almost become a purely geometrical form of decoration. Material 0.197″ sheet steel. Diameter 17″. Surface finish: natural colour of the material, decoration gilded.

Dish with a wide rim, diameter 12.5″, forged from 0.118″ thick sheet steel. Coat of arms and grooves chiselled, coloured, lacquered and gilded.

Hammered bronze dish 0.118″ thick, diameter 20.5″, gives a bell-like ring when struck.
Right-hand page: the same dish seen from above.

Hammered brass dish with a tall foot, semi-matt finish produced by brushing, diameter 18″.

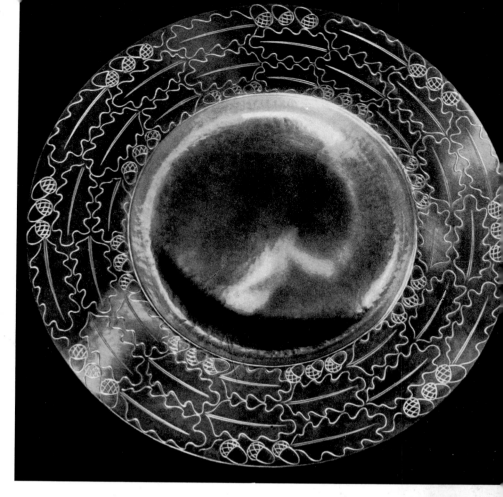

Copper dish, bright finish produced by brushing. Decoration: oak foliage, grooved.

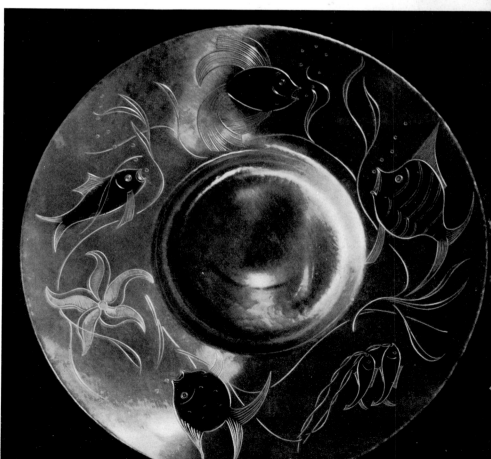

Copper dish, matt finish produced by brushing, the body surfaces of the fish highly polished.

Dish "frozen movement".
Forged from steel and coated with molten copper.

Steel dish with forged in copper ring.
Diameter 6.5″.

Wrought iron dish, 0.236″ thick, greatest width 17″, gilded with pure gold leaf and rubbed, so that the gold only remains visible in the hollows and pores. The monogram in the middle is done on so small a scale that it needs to be sought and discovered. For a closer description see the introduction.

Left-hand page:
Copper dish with artificially
produced patina.

Candelabrum, forged from
one piece of steel, apart
from the drip dishes. This
candelabrum contains the
thickening, branching and
tapering features that are
also the basic elements in
the natural form, as the
study photographed with
it shows.

Large hammered copper dish, slightly curved. Wall plate standing in front of it with ornate chiselled decoration, theme "Water". Surface finish: burnt black by fire, animal bodies and hammered edge rubbed bright. Detail drawing of the wall plate.

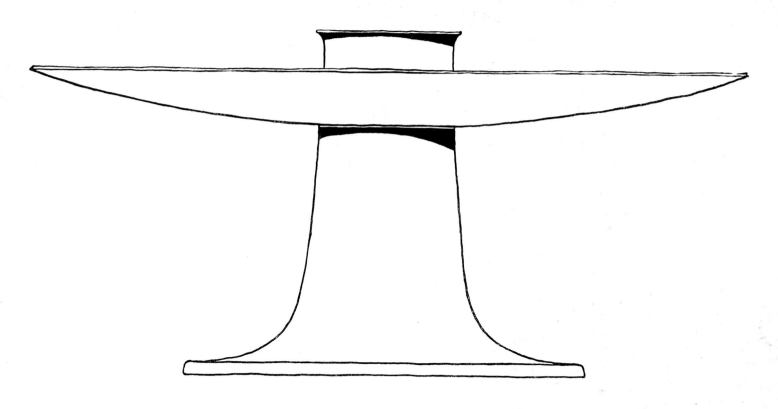

Candlestick, forged from steel, bright
finish produced by treatment with
acid.
Above: working drawing.

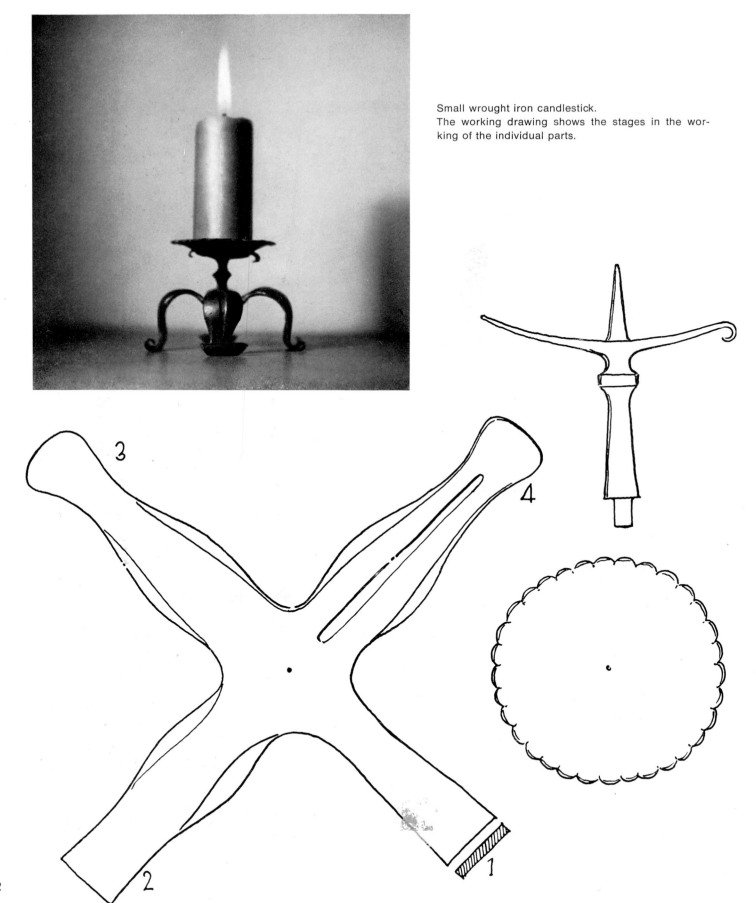

Small wrought iron candlestick.
The working drawing shows the stages in the working of the individual parts.

Small wrought iron candlestick with handle. Both the four-part foot and the handle forged from one piece.

The left-hand page above and below shows a comparison of Nature and the work of man. A tulip is drawn at three stages of flowering. Studies from Nature are necessary, not so that we can imitate her, but so that we can observe and divine her laws. From the basic shape of the tulip — expressing opening and catching — are evolved with a few supplementary lines a cup, a bowl, a dish, a candlestick. The implements are an embodiment of Nature and yet are far from being a mere imitation of her.

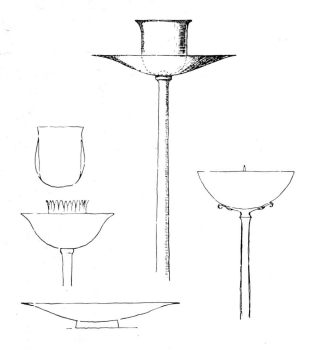

Right-hand page:
My "grandmother's candlestick". Doesn't it remind us of the candlesticks our grandmothers had standing on their bedside tables? How functional it was and yet at the same time well designed. It had a large base and so it could not fall over easily. There was a handle to hold it by, the candle was held firmly in the socket, you did not even have to look for the matches, because there was room for the box in the base and if a bad candle was used the wax could run down as much as it liked, without spoiling the table or the cloth. Nor did the candlestick break if it was knocked or fell over, because it was made of metal. This implement was a true servant of man.

Candlestick made of strong brass tubing, drip dish spun, not hammered, polished semi-matt.

Heavy iron candlestick, diameter of the foot 6.3″. The slits relieve the heaviness of the candlestick.

Forged candlestick, 14″ tall, shaft and foot worked from one piece, see also page 39.

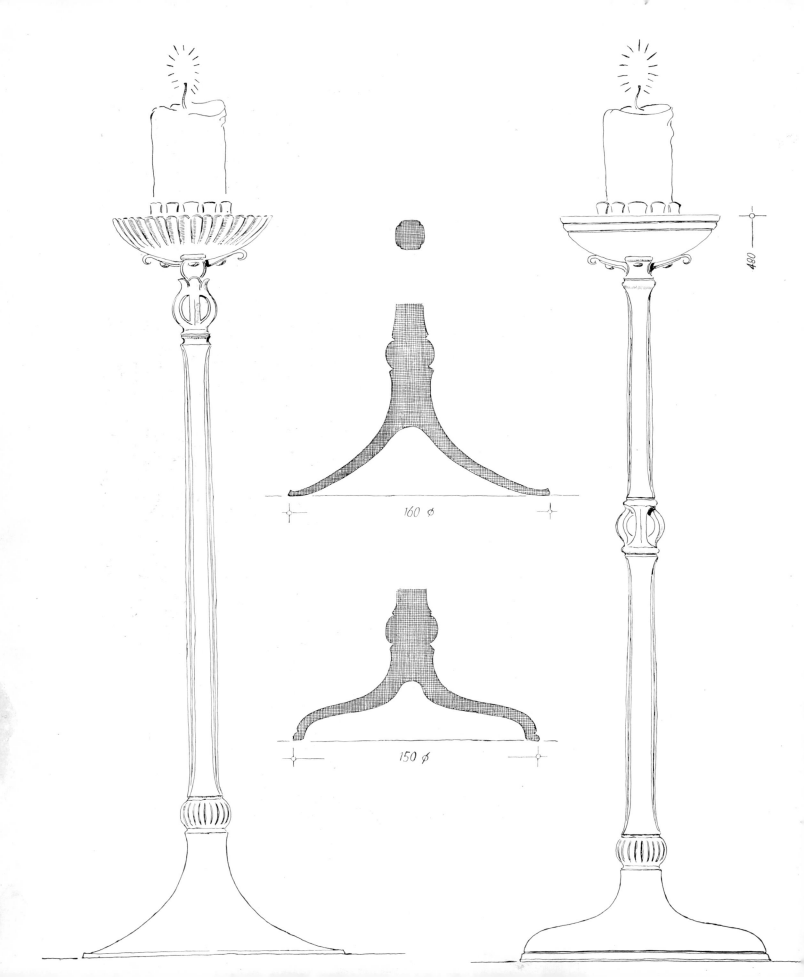

160 ⌀

150 ⌀

480

Two tall candlesticks, slightly varying in form, shaft and foot forged from one piece, see drawing on left-hand page. The imposing effect is increased by gilding with gold leaf.

Right-hand page:
Candlestick on mosaic table, polished marble.

Left:
Candelabrum, gilded with gold leaf and lacquered. The upward-pointing arms relieved by twisting the material.

Below:
Tall candlestick, shaft opened up, gilded with gold leaf and the outer surfaces rubbed.

Family candelabrum. Apart from the drip dishes and coats of arms with chiselled monograms, this candle-stick is forged from one piece.

Heavy wrought iron candlestick.

Children's candlesticks that are always used on birthdays will accompany them throughout their whole lives and keep alive the memory of childhood into old age. This fact gives us an obligation to avoid experimental and transitional solutions when fashioning such implements and to give them a timeless form. We want to send the children on their way with an appreciation of plainness, simplicity and clarity; for taste must be educated from the cradle.

Candlesticks for a boy and a girl.

Right-hand page:
Preliminary drawings for nine different children's candlesticks, tree-like, the spherical forged base representing the earth, the shaft like a trunk tapering towards the top, either twisted or opened up, in another case upset in the middle, or upset in two places, grooved or profiled, the drip dish at the top and the socket forming the crown, and yet purely functional. The basic form is the same throughout. Next to the forged inscription (name and date of birth) are chiselled various decorations taken from life, see details on the left.

Where there are several children in a family, those who cannot yet read their names are thereby in a position to recognize their own candlestick by its shape. Such a candlestick can contribute towards the child's learning at an early age to appreciate such basic changes in shape as thickening, twisting, dividing etc. — processes that occur in Nature.

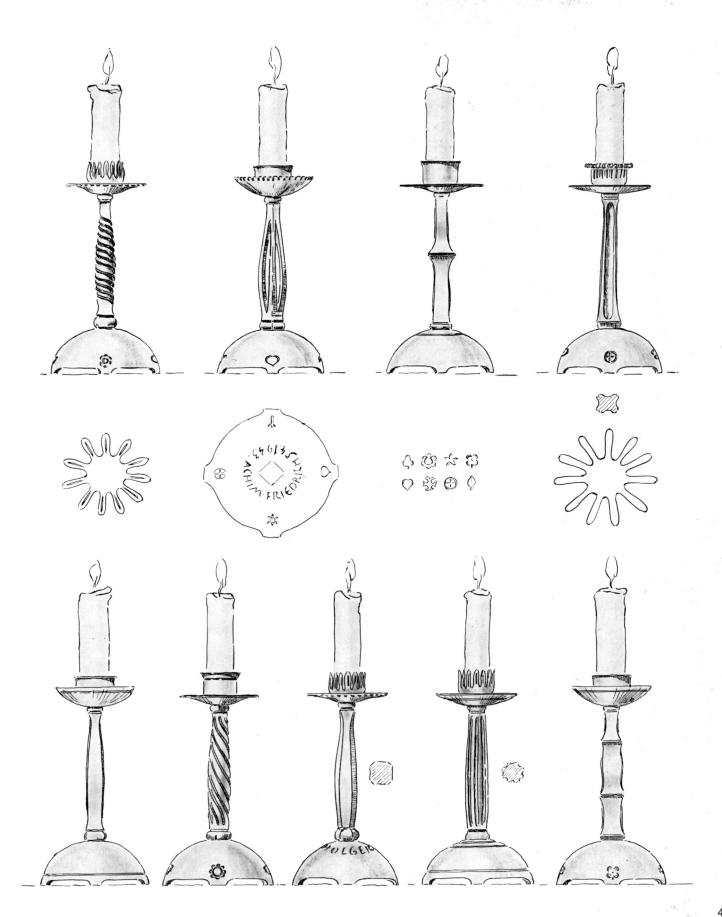

Standing candlestick of functional design for a church.
The tripod (see right-hand page) is forged from one
piece, shaft of 2.36″ thick square-sectioned steel bar,
profiled, tapering towards the top and opened out.
The four curled scrolls created in this way hold the
large grooved dish.

Left: five-branched standing candlestick, the branches attached by fire welding, four-part foot.

Below: standing candelabrum with three candles, see working drawing for it on the right-hand page.

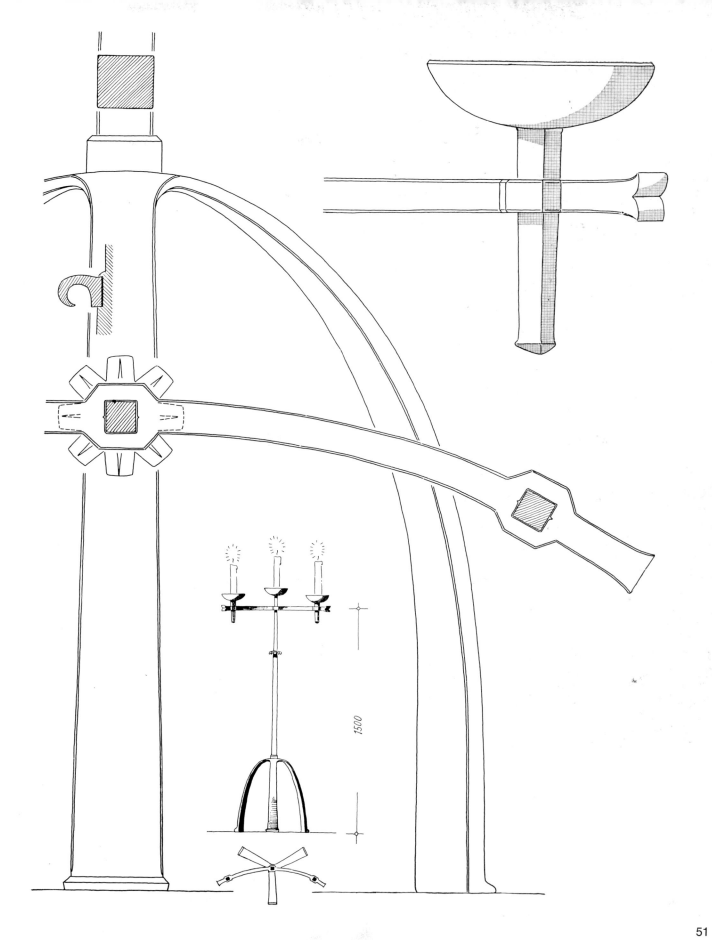

1500

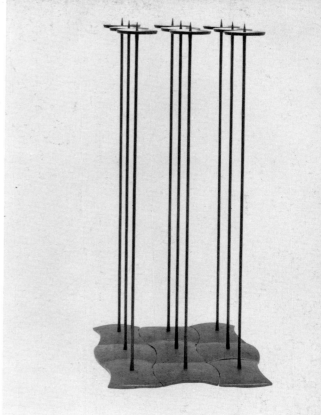

Standing candlesticks 4′3″ tall, forged in steel, with black finish and brass top pieces, as festive illumination. The three illustrations show some of the many possibilities for grouping.

Left-hand page:
Part view of a group of large standing candlesticks for a church. The main parts are made from large steel plates, all surfaces worked.

Altar candlestick.
The candlestick is forged from one piece. The grooves worked into the outer surfaces, heightening the soaring effect, show the forging process clearly. They widen the material and this in turn is necessary for the candlestick to stand firmly. See also right-hand picture.

Steel candlestick, not forged,
but turned on a lathe. The
grooves with a matt finish, the
surfaces bright.

Right-hand page:
steel cross with working drawing, polished semi-matt.

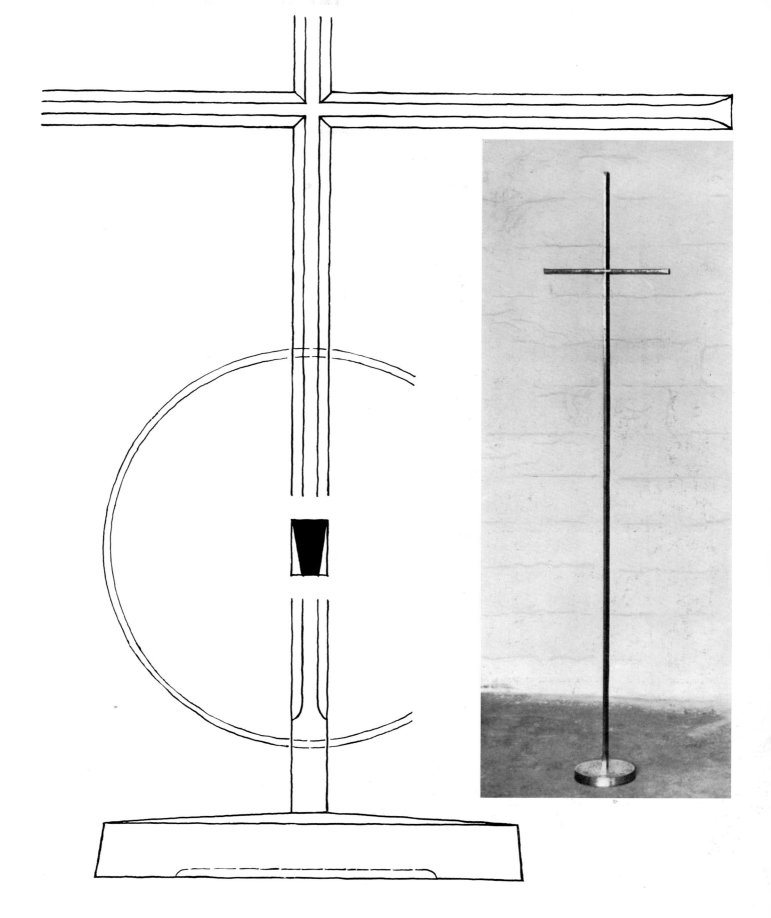

Altar cross. Working drawing on the right-hand page.
Cross and matching candlesticks forged in steel and
coated with copper over heat.

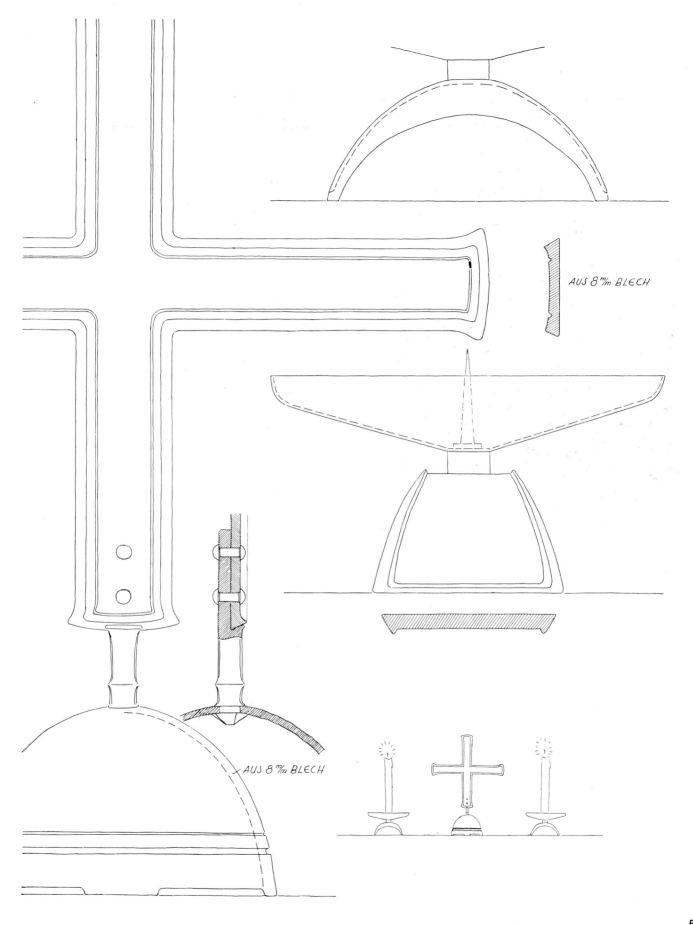

AUS 8ᵐᵐ BLECH

AUS 8ᵐᵐ BLECH

Holy-water stoup made from copper by raising and forging.

Right-hand page:
Baptismal dish of hammered copper, the chiselled inscription with artificially produced green patina.

View through to the baptistry.

60

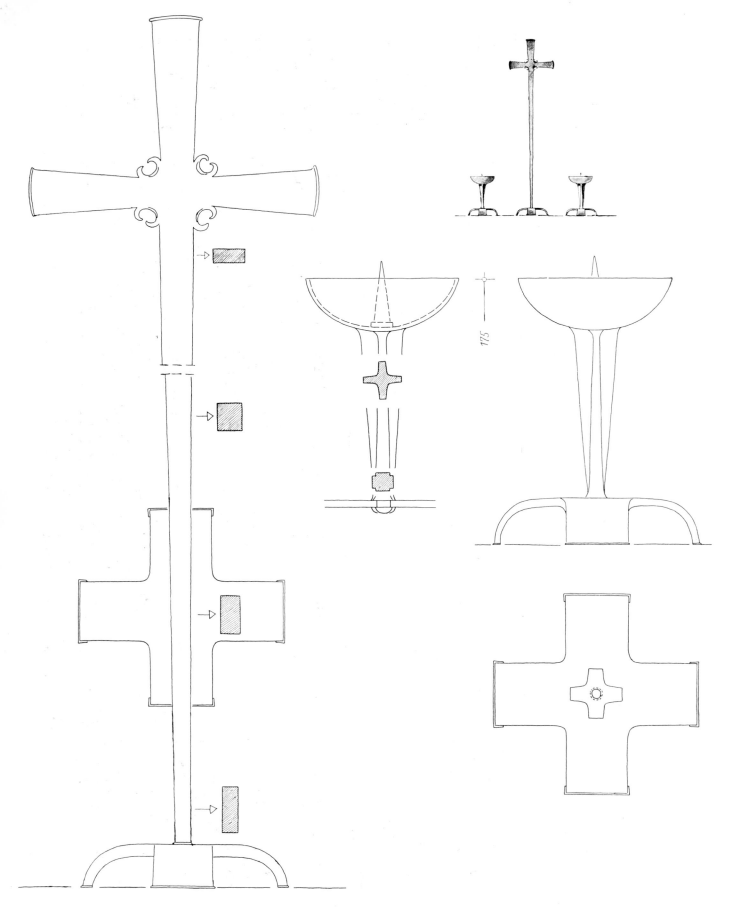

Cross with matching candlesticks. Cross forged from one piece, foot riveted in.
Left: working drawing.

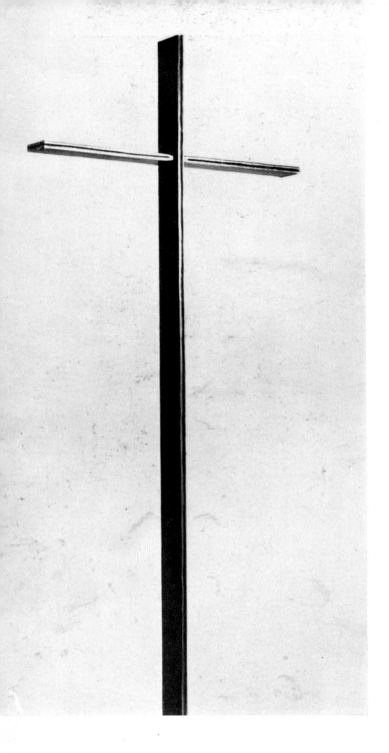

Cross of flat bar-steel set with narrow edges on face, the grooves on the front surfaces are hand done.

Grave cross of square-sectioned iron bar, the terminations opened out from the solid bar and forged. Ring of flat bar-steel riveted on. Inscription chiselled and gilded.

Memorial plate of 0.315″ thick sheet steel, edge hammered, inscription forged deeply and gilded with gold leaf.

Old grave cross in a churchyard in Tyrol.

Grave cross. The vertical flat iron bar is in one piece and forged into an angle at the back so that the cross bar is held firmly, visible riveting. The ornamentations with the milkwort flowers are opened out from the cross bar and are made from one piece. Name deeply forged and gilded.

Memorial plate of 0.394″ sheet steel.

Cross on a church roof, 15′ tall, the greatest width 6′10″, of flat bar-iron 1.575″×0.786″ or 1.575×0.472 the ball of sheet copper, diameter 25″.

DONA NOBIS PACEM

IHS

OSKAR KRAUSE
+ 29.3.1896
+ 30.8.1915

ULRICH HORN
+ 18.9.1918
+ 8.12.1942

EDZARD WIESINGER
+ 22.10.1907
+ 12.8.1944

JOH.15.5.

Drawing on the right-hand page: Inscription forged in bronze for a grave stone (boulder).

GUSTAV EBNER
* 1.6.1866 † 6.4.1944.

JOHANNES HÜLSEN
* 13.4.1887 † 10.9.1944.

887 † 10.

$\frac{6}{6}$ RESP. $\frac{8}{8}$

$\frac{13}{6} \neq$

EHRENMITGLIEDER
DES
DEUTSCHEN THEATERS

ALBERT BASSERMANN
GERTRUD EYSOLDT
LUCIE HÖFLICH
GERDA MÜLLER
W. NEMIROWITSCH-DANTSCHENKO
K.S. STANISLAWSKIY
PAUL WEGENER
EDUARD v. WINTERSTEIN
WILLY A. KLEINAU
KARL RUPPERT
ERNST BUSCH

Commemorative plaque in the lobby of the German theatre in Berlin. Wood covered with light-coloured leather, inscription forged in copper, brownish-green artificially produced patina.

Right-hand page:
Inscription forged from flat bar-steel, 1.97″ × 0.472″ above the entrance to a cemetery chapel.

UND
SIE
LEBEN
DOCH

Inscribed plaque 0.315″ thick, the edge more strongly hammered at the corners.

DER
MENSCHHEIT
WÜRDE IST
IN EURE
HAND GEGE
BEN · BEWAH
RET SIE · SIE
SINKT MIT EUCH
MIT EUCH WIRD
SIE SICH
HEBEN

Left: inscribed plaque of 0.394″ thick sheet steel, size 1′9″×2′7″, edge hammered, inscription and laurel deeply forged, leaf surfaces coated in part with molten copper and brass, the copper berries forged in. The whole plaque treated with acid to produce a bright finish.

Above: Enlarged section of this plaque.

Inscribed plaque of 0.315″ copper for the memorial in the ruins of the Aegidien Church in Hanover. The background of the inscription is deeply forged. The craftsman's work on the surface is clearly visible in the illustration on the right-hand page.

Copper plaque 0.315″ thick, made for the same ruin. Chronicle and ground-plan of the former church both deeply forged.

KRIEG UND KATASTROPHE
FORDERTEN DAS LEBEN
VIELER EINWOHNER UNSERER
STADT AN DER FRONT
UND IN DER HEIMAT
12628 FIELEN 1914-1918
1939-1945 FIELEN 11360
7000 WURDEN VON BOMBEN
GETÖTET · 6700 WERDEN
VERMISST · UNZÄHLIGE STARBEN
IN LAGERN IN GEFÄNGNISSEN
UND AUF DER FLUCHT ·

Wall plate of 0.394″ thick copper
for the Oliva Square in Berlin.
The emblem of the monastery
church of Oliva is brought into
relief by forging the surrounding
material more deeply, brownish-
green artificially produced patina.

Right-hand page:
Detail from it.

Town coat of arms, forged in the
form of grids. Fixed to an old
public building.

Wrought iron sign for a greengrocer's shop in a small town.

Sketch of an old sign at the hotel "Zur Post" in Nuremberg.

Sign for a hairdresser's shop, the bowl of the hanging part made of raised sheet brass.

Firm's sign, tendril and letters gilded with gold leaf.

Architecturally suitable inn sign in a town in South Germany.

Right:
Old farrier's sign. The use of the horseshoe shape in the hanging part is unusual.

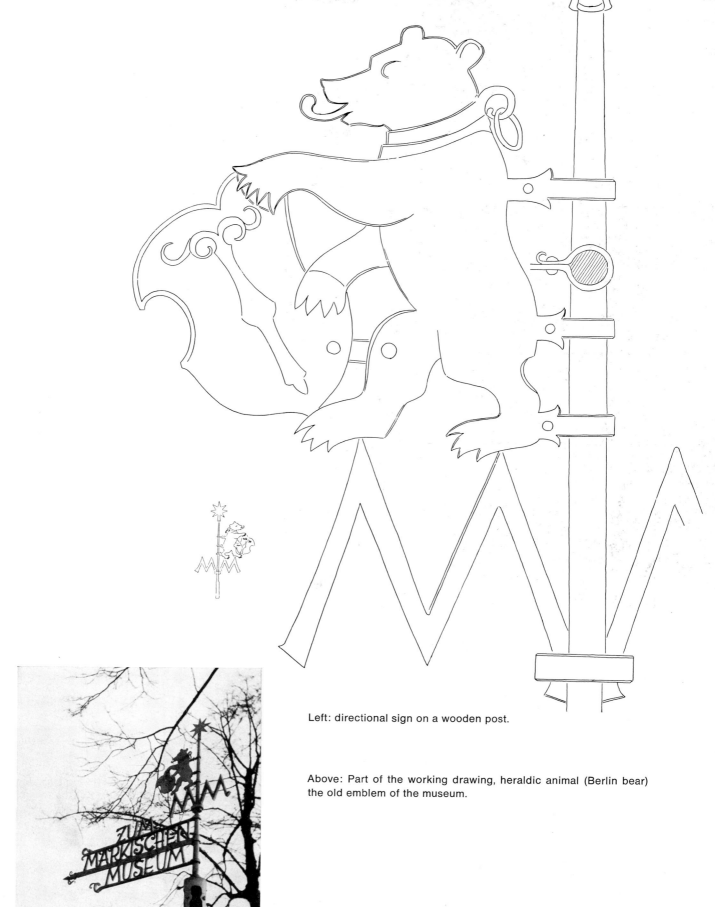

Left: directional sign on a wooden post.

Above: Part of the working drawing, heraldic animal (Berlin bear) the old emblem of the museum.

Spider in web.
Wall decoration for an entrance hall.

Wall decoration "scorpion", the sign of the zodiac of the master of the house.

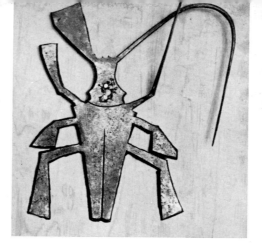

Stages in the working of the beetle, as can be seen, forged from one piece.

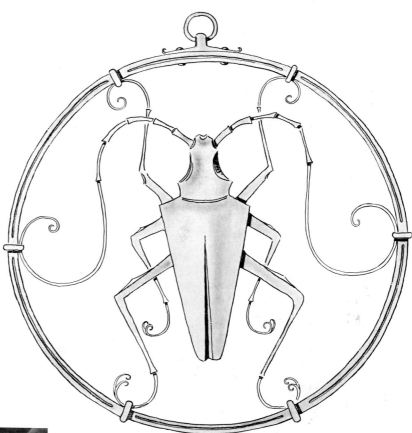

Forging the beetle.

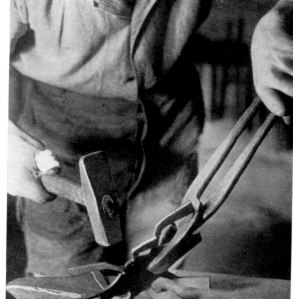

Preliminary drawing of the wall decoration "beetle". The feelers and legs are not worked naturalistically and serve to fasten it by. The body is therefore not plastic, but on the same plane as the framework and the sculptural part (the delicate feelers and legs as opposed to the flat body) only hinted at. The typical characteristics of the little beetle are thereby not only preserved but heightened.

Wall decoration for a stairway with figured representations of the three elements: Air — Water — Earth — and painting one of them.

Right-hand page:
Large wall decoration "Water". The symbolically represented plant is opened up from the frame, the fish are each forged from one piece of material.

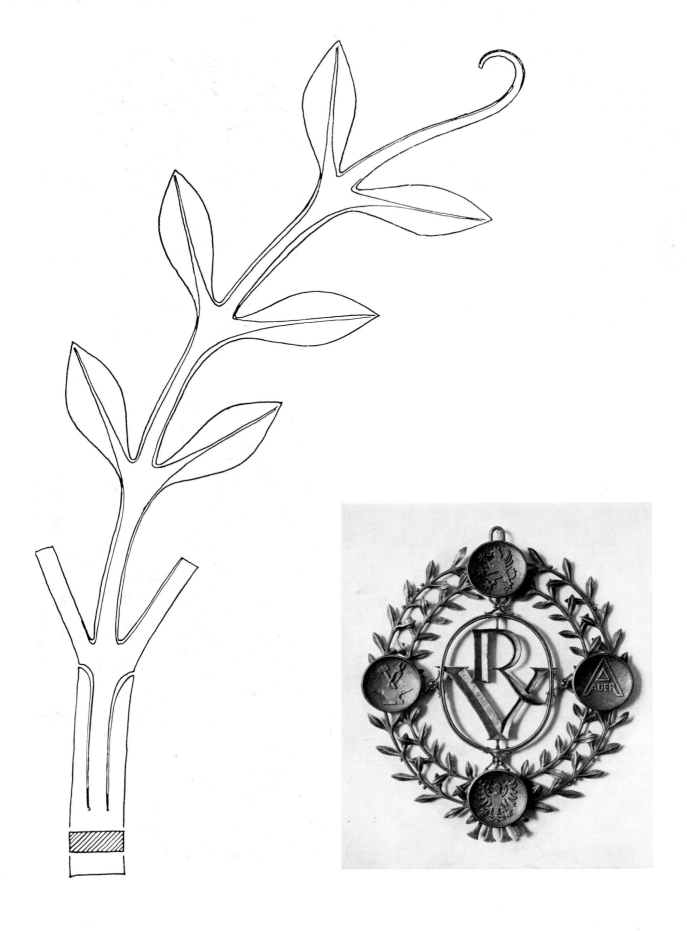

Left-hand page: forged wall decoration, jubilee presentation, see also description in the introduction page 8. The sketch shows how the laurel branches were made from one flat bar of iron by opening up and hammering.

Above and right: Details from this wall decoration.

Gargoyle on a well.

Below: Sketch for gargoyle, fish made of raised sheet copper.

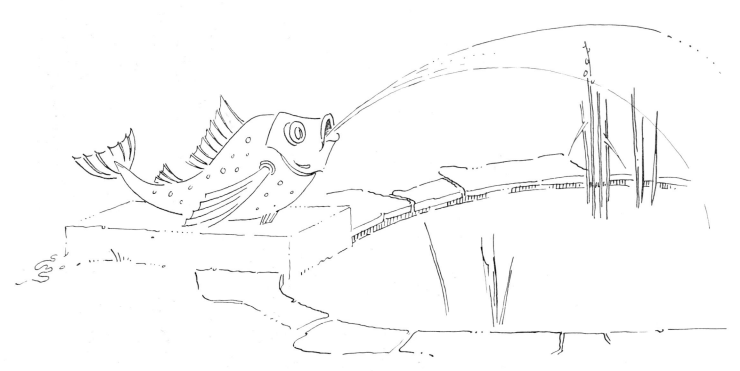

90

Old well in Salzburg, roof of copper, diamond-shaped trellis work of round iron bars. The intersections of the front bars with the back ones are of particular interest.

Detail from the well illustrated above.

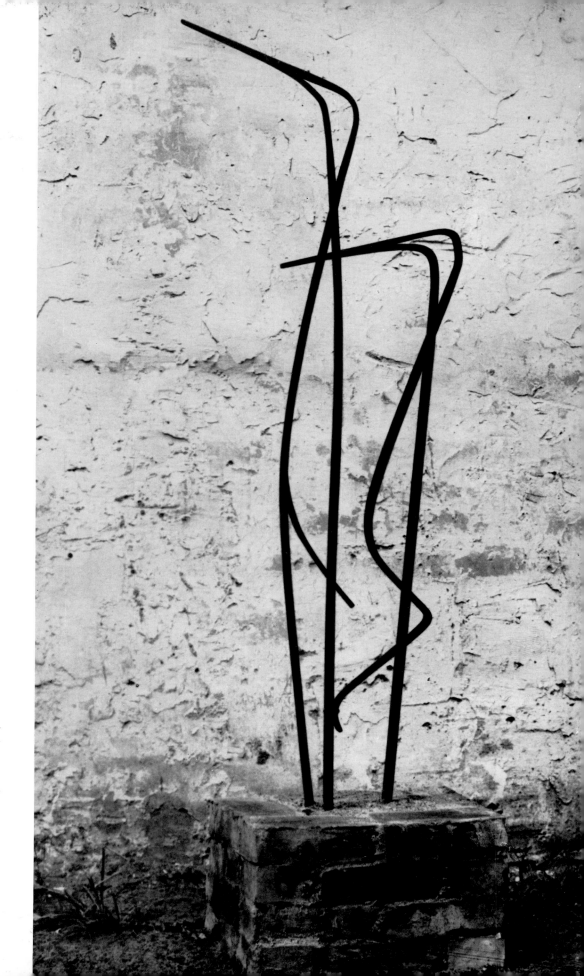

Figures with both graphic and plastic effect, "Cranes", forged in copper.

Left-hand page: water-spewing fish made of raised sheet copper to relieve the edge of a pool.

Preliminary sketch of the fountain top illustrated on the
right-hand page, gilded copper.

Above and below:
Gay crowning pieces forged in iron.

Right:
Sketch of an old crowning piece on the roof of a Tirolean farm-house.

Right-hand page:
Working drawing for two boot scrapers forged as figures.

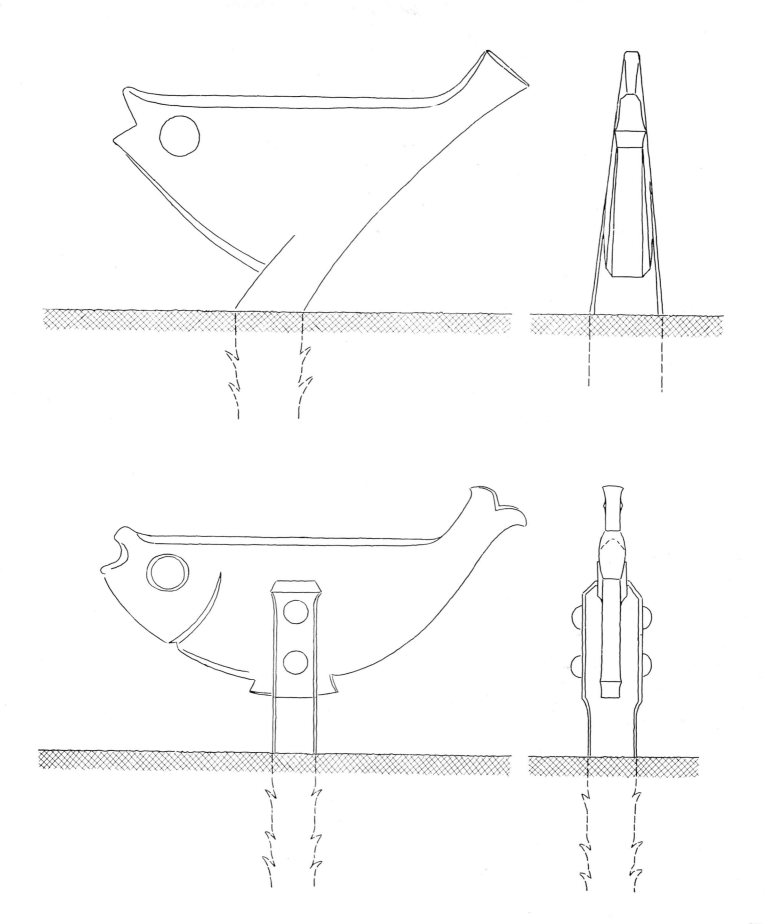

Wrought iron clock dial.

Part view of the same.

Clock dial on a small clock tower, coloured finish, figures and
hands gilded with gold leaf.

Left-hand page:
Working drawing of a clock dial. The hands and symbols of the zodiac are brass, polished bright, the remainder is iron with a black finish.

Clock dial on an outside wall.

Wrought iron clock with signs of the zodiac. The hands, that are worked in brass, bear symbols of the sun and moon.

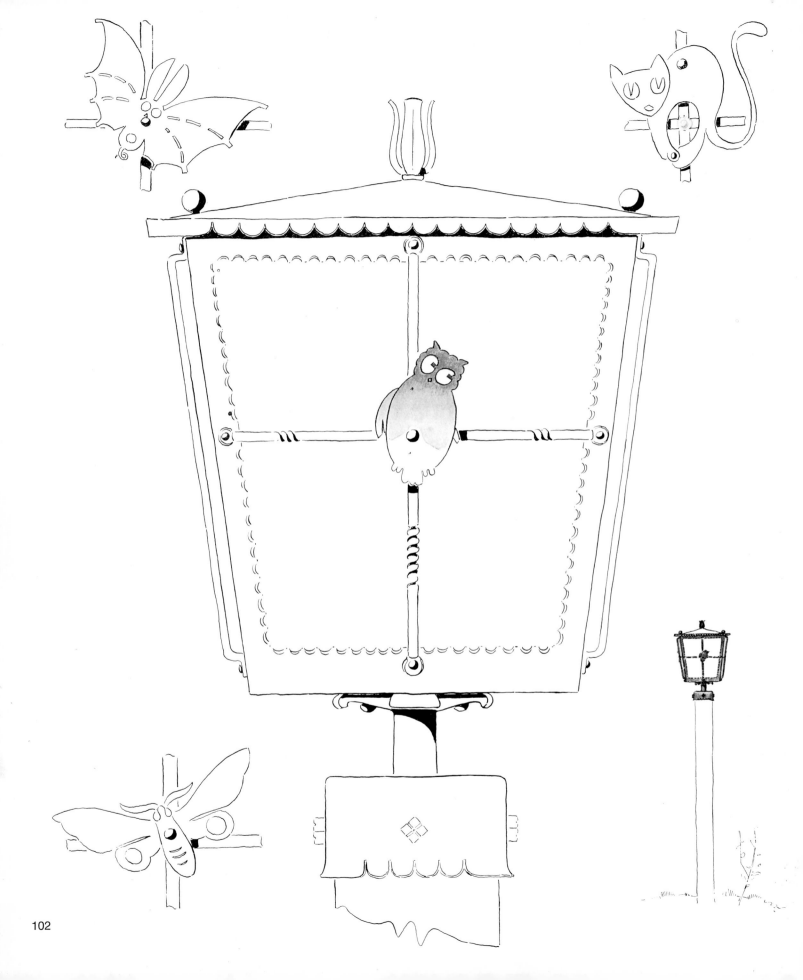

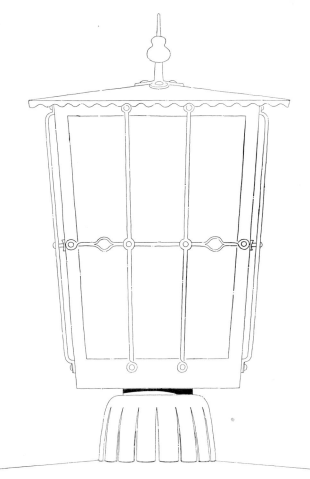

Design for a lamp on a gate post.

Working drawing of a lantern on a bracket at the entrance of a house.

Garden lamp on a wooden post. The lamp looks even gayer when it is alight as the amusing little animals show up as silhouettes.

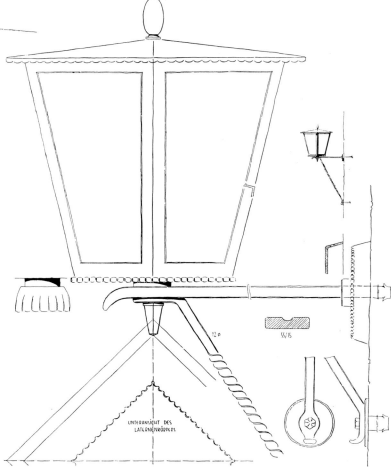

Wall lamp with fish.

Wall lamp on a country church with working drawing illustrated on the right-hand page.

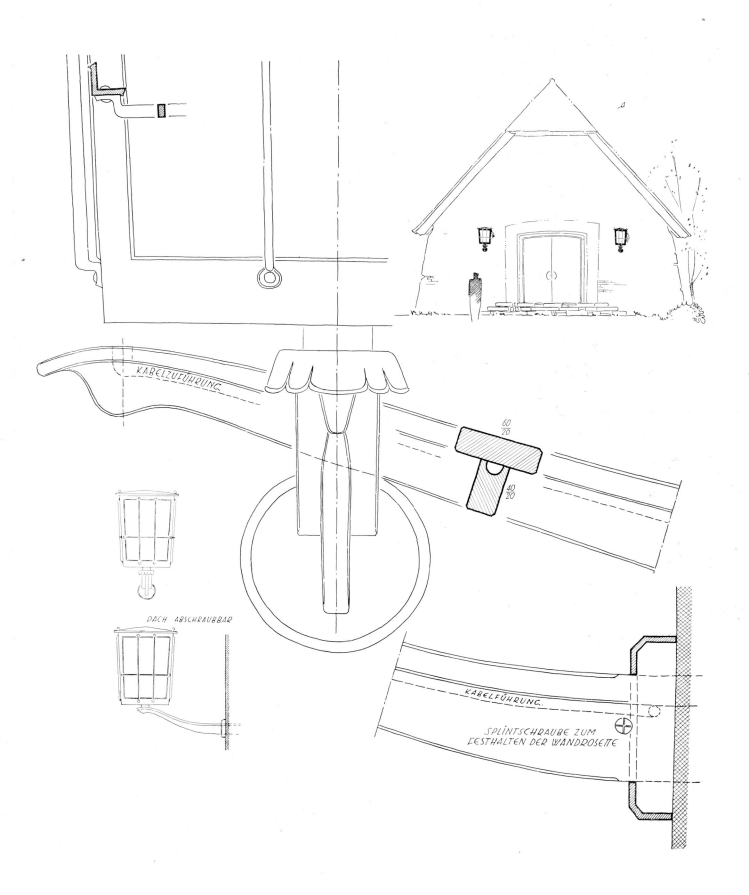

KABELZUFÜHRUNG

60/20

40/20

DACH ABSCHRAUBBAR

KABELFÜHRUNG.

SPLINTSCHRAUBE ZUM
FESTHALTEN DER WANDROSETTE

Lamp with tendrils above an entrance.

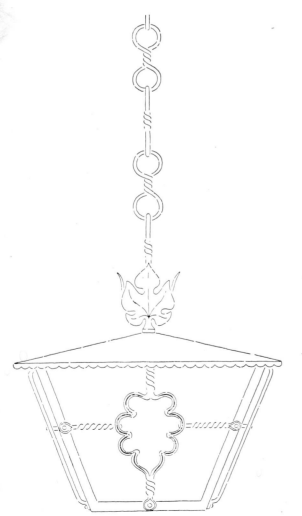

Left and right-hand page:
Preliminary drawings of hanging lamps for inns.

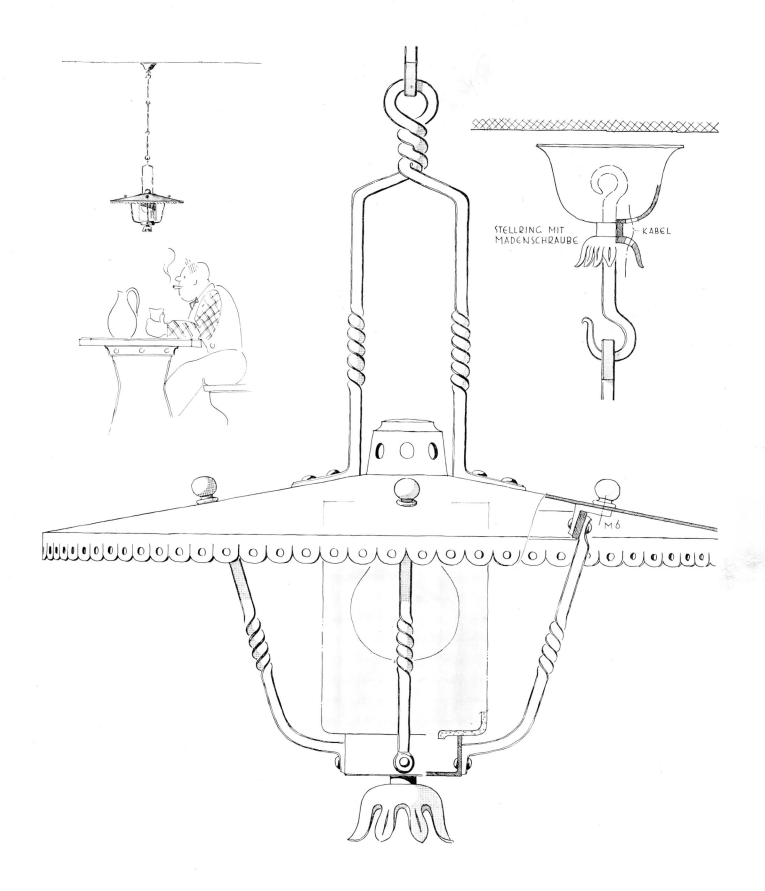

STELLRING MIT
MADENSCHRAUBE

KABEL

M6

GLAS

GUMMIPLÄTTCHEN

58 ø

2800

108

Lamp standards on the terrace of a school.

Left-hand page:
Preliminary and working drawings for them. Each lamp has a different motif.

Lighting appliances on the façade of an old Berlin building in the Unter den Linden Street. The steel part with a white finish on the inside, the bright brass sockets and the pearl bulbs are visible through the clear glass.

Hanging lamp made for an old palace. Iron with a coloured finish, the fitments in the middle are brass, the narrow glass panels are facet-cut crystal.

Right: Old baroque lamp made of bronze.

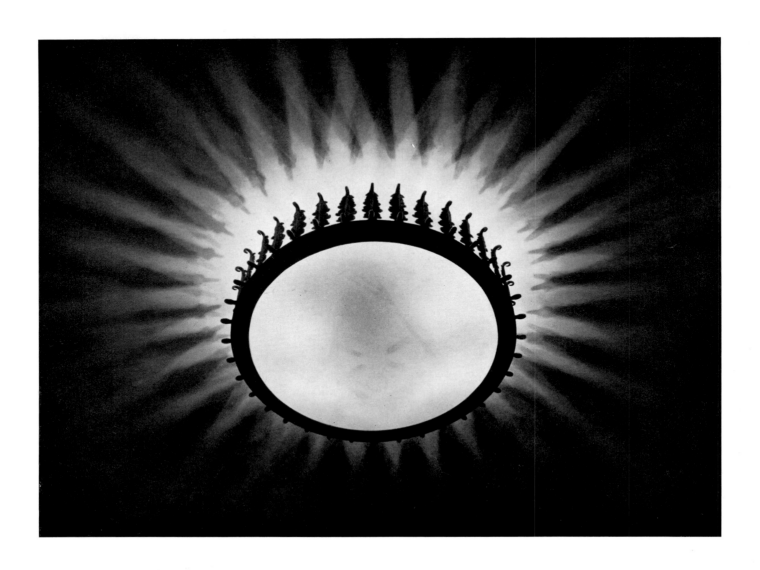

Various ceiling-lights.

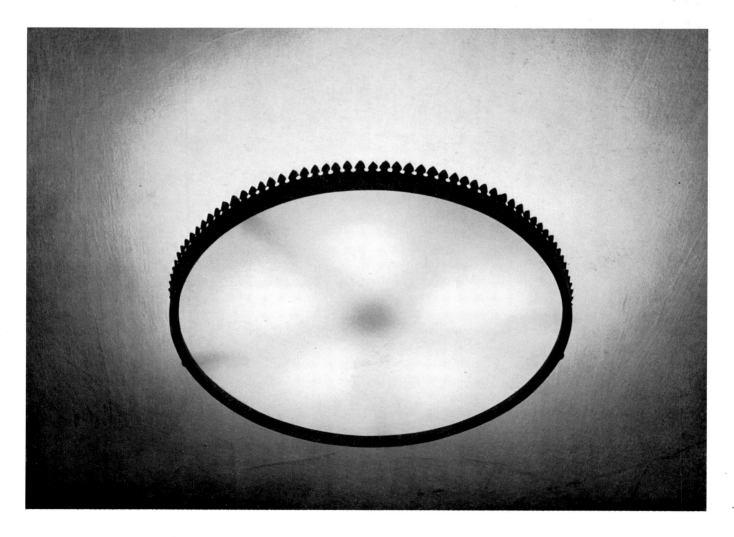

Part view of a tiled table. The leg forged from one piece with a double fastening.

Wrought iron table with glass mosaic, white and gold. The leg fastenings are of particular interest, see the working drawing and detail on the right-hand page. The leaves formed into the ball are different on all four legs.

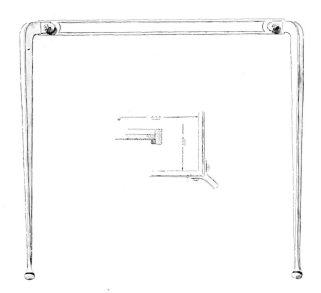

Small iron table with visibly attached legs. Working drawing.

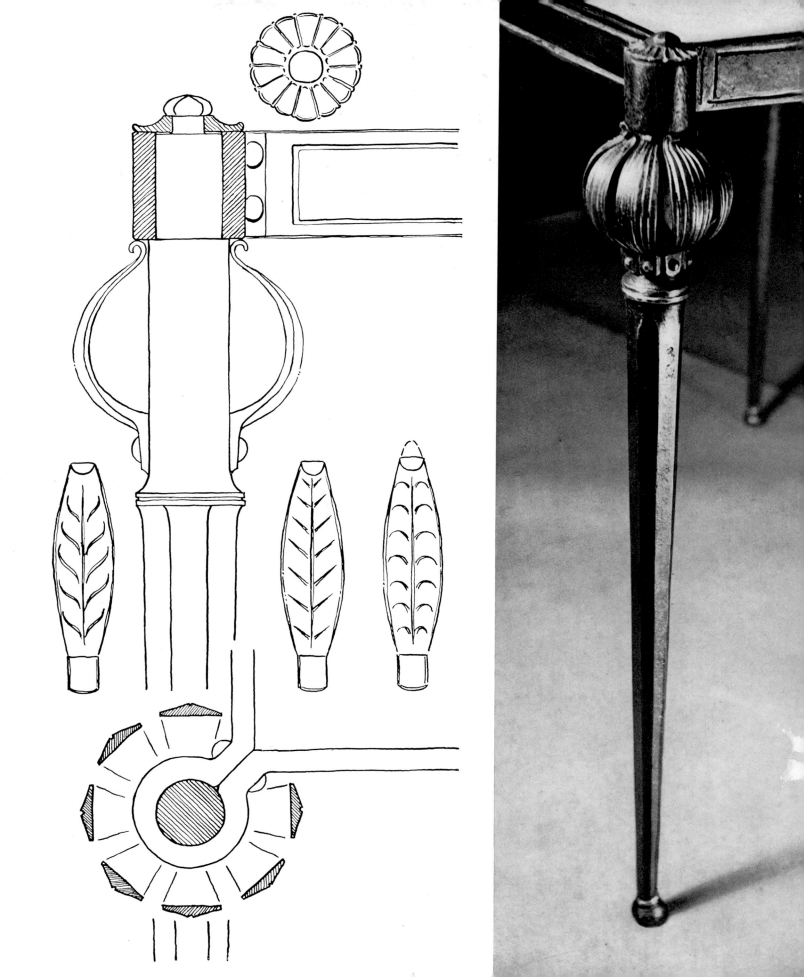

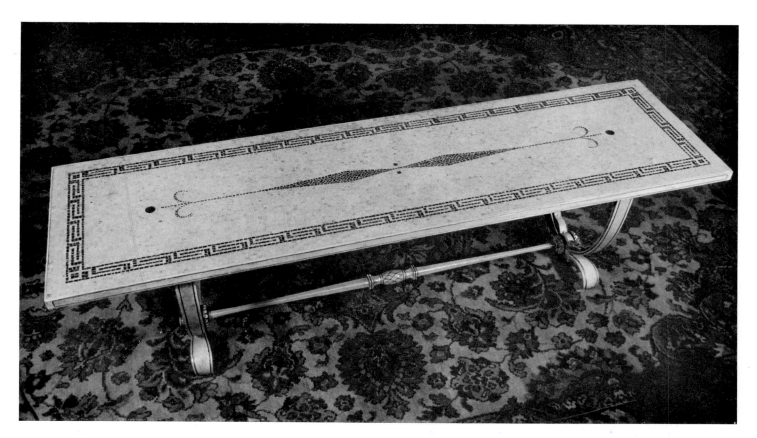

Long iron table, white and gold mosaic, iron with a light-coloured finish, partly gilded.

Mosaic table.

Left: Iron table with marble mosaic, legs opened up and twisted with reinforcements at the bottom.

Left:
Iron table with ornate edge, black with gilded grooves, mosaic top, white and grey.
Standard lamp, iron, gilded with gold leaf and lacquered.

Garden furniture of round steel bar, sprayed white.

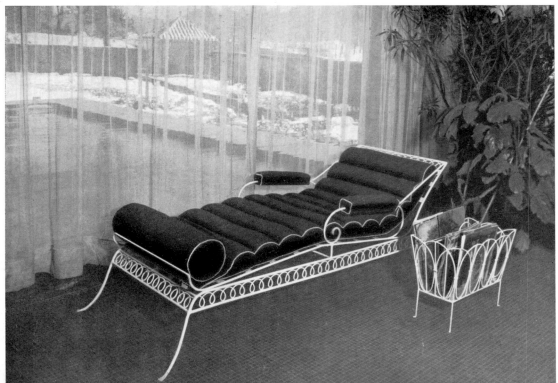

Left-hand page and above:
Furniture of round steel bar for a conservatory.
Design: Geyer-Raack.

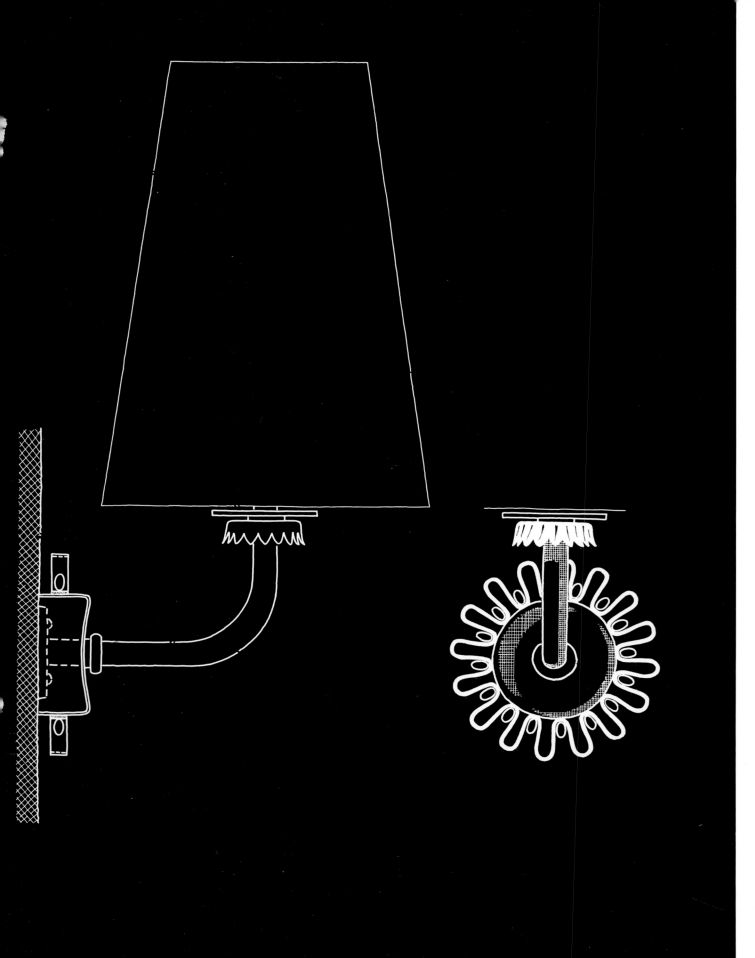

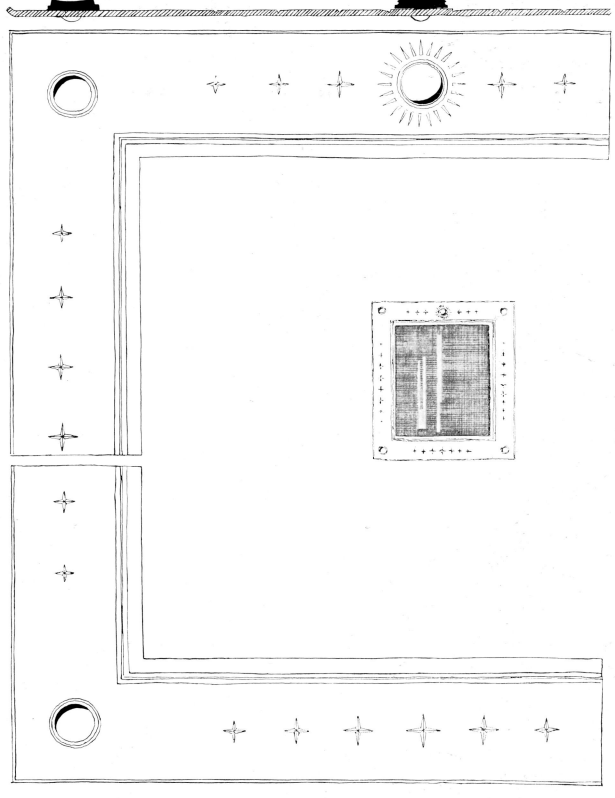

Wide mirror frame with light-coloured finish, the mounted concave and convex studs (see section above) are polished brass.

Left-hand page: Small hall-light with light-coloured finish, the wavy edging and rosette of leaves are polished brass.

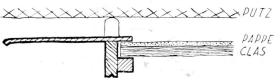

PUTZ

PAPPE
CLAS

Right-hand page:
Working drawings for various coat hooks attached to a rail or bar.

Coat hooks, forged from one piece.

Drawing of a coat hook, iron with a light-coloured finish, ball at the top of brass, polished.

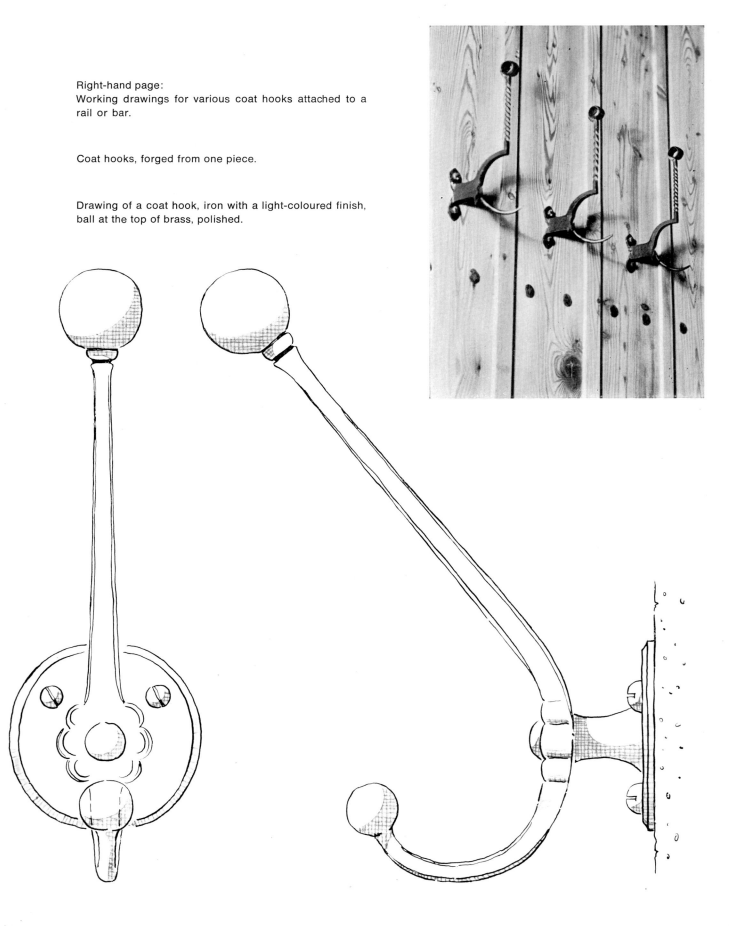

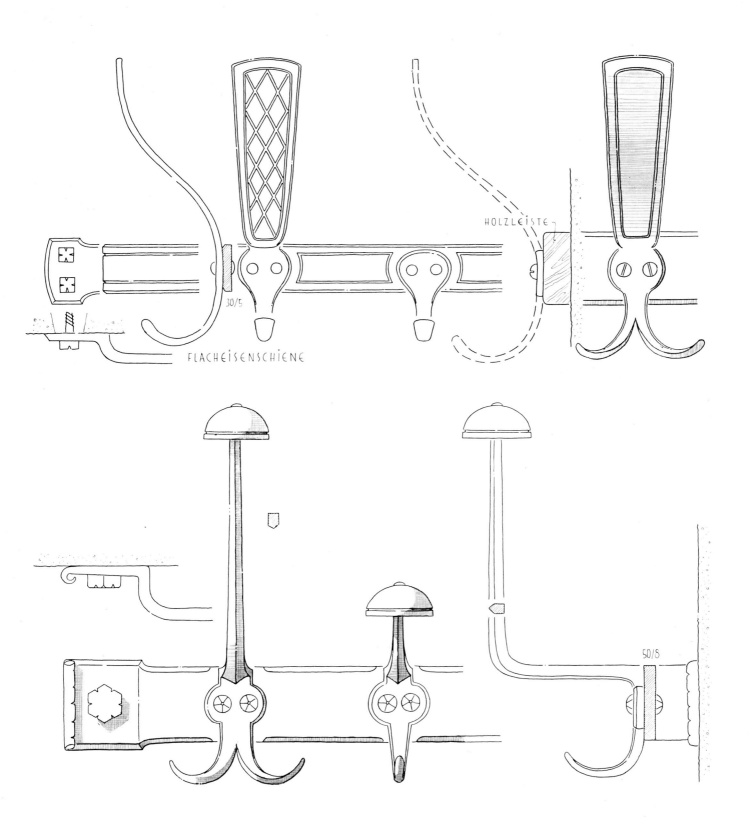

FLACHEISENSCHIENE

HOLZLEISTE

30/S

50/S

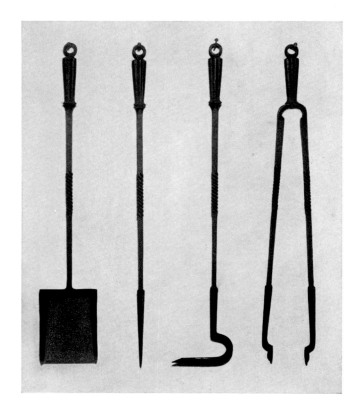

Fire irons on a chimney wall.

Poker, forged in one piece.

Top part of a grate support.
The globe is forged from one square sectioned
iron bar.

Fire dog with bars of the grate.

Grate with detail.

Grate with detail, the ball in the crowning piece is brass.

Grate support. The small scrolls are opened out from the solid bar.

Forging the grate support.

Right-hand page: grate support. The crown was made by opening up the solid bar.

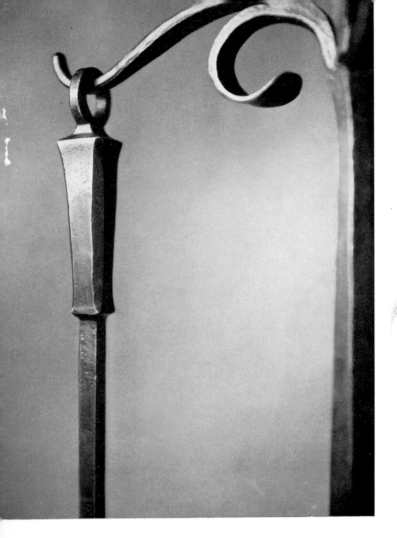

Right-hand page:
Working drawing of a fire iron stand
and the implements belonging to it.

Fire iron stand with implements and details from them.

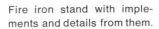

132

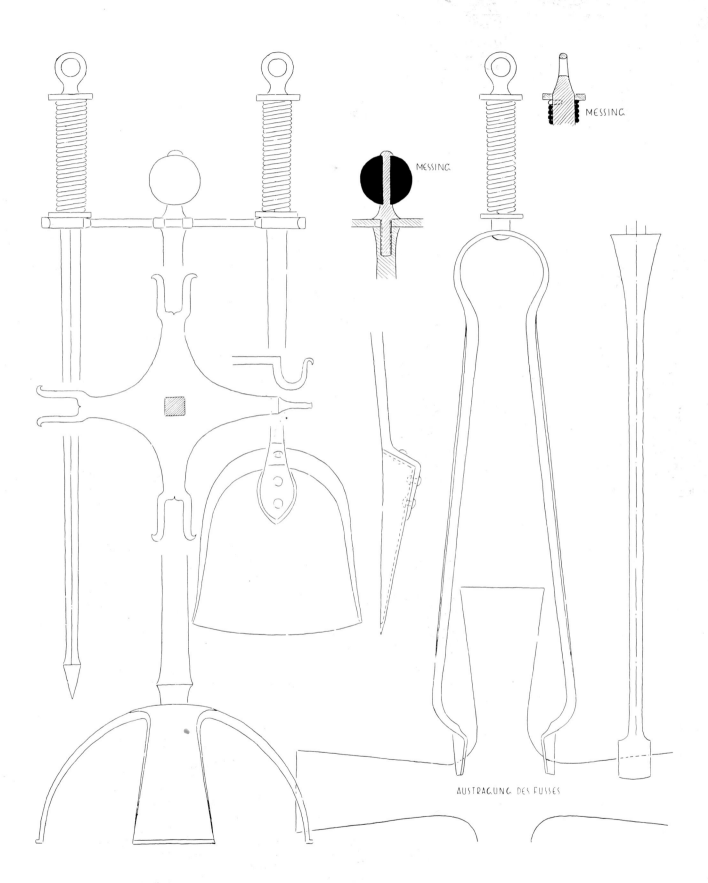

MESSING

MESSING

AUSTRAGUNG DES FUSSES

133

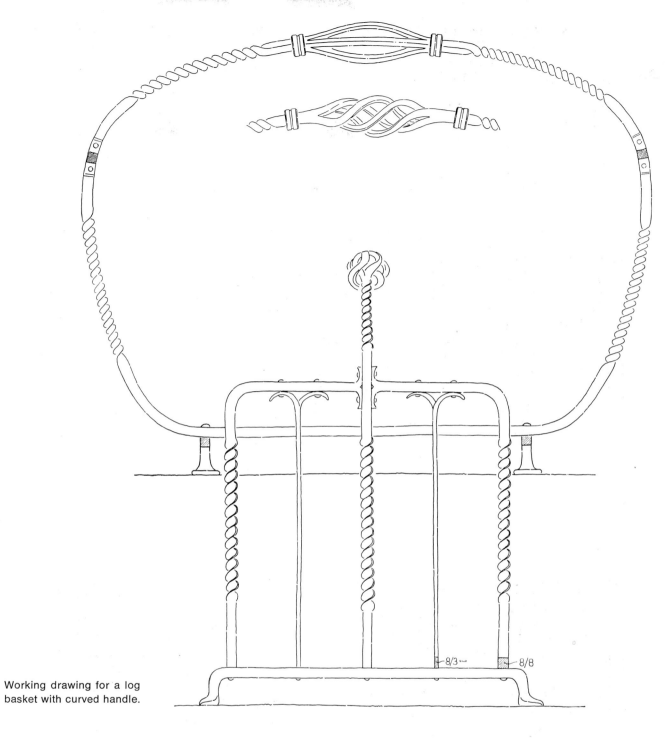

Working drawing for a log
basket with curved handle.

8/3 — 8/8

Wrought iron log basket for a hearth.
Left-hand page: details from it.

Various furniture mountings.

Right-hand page: forged lock and handle mounting for a wooden door.

Oak chest with ornate iron mounting.
The front opens downwards.

Key forged from one piece, the dog as the symbol of the guardian is both handle and support.

Right-hand page:
Detail of one of the bottom hinges with sectional drawing and reproductions of some of the differently shaped ornamental nails.

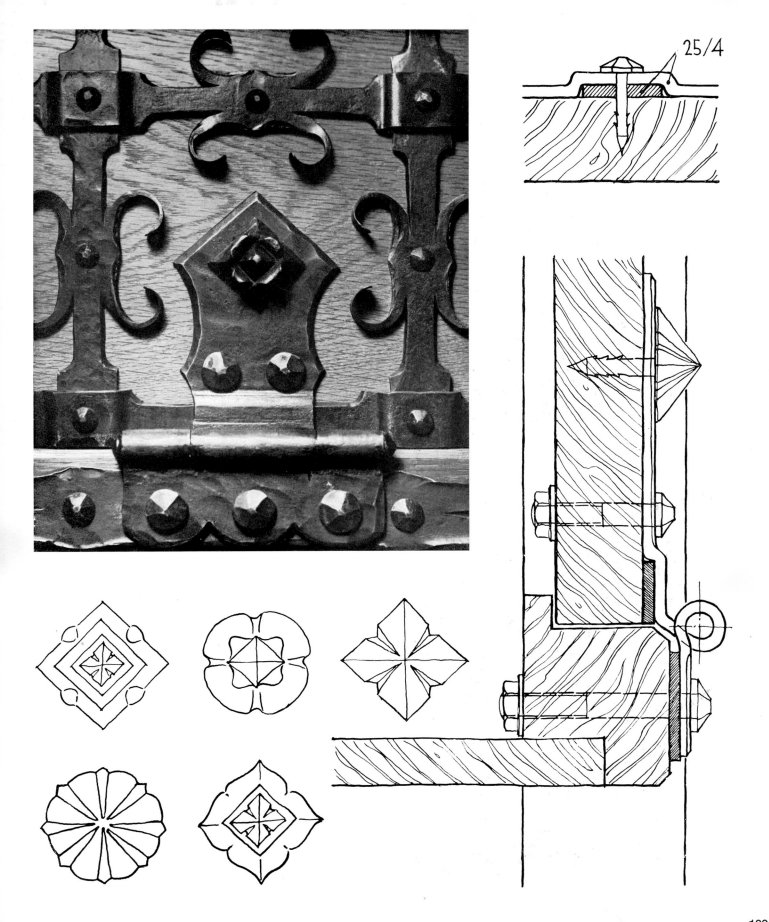

25/4

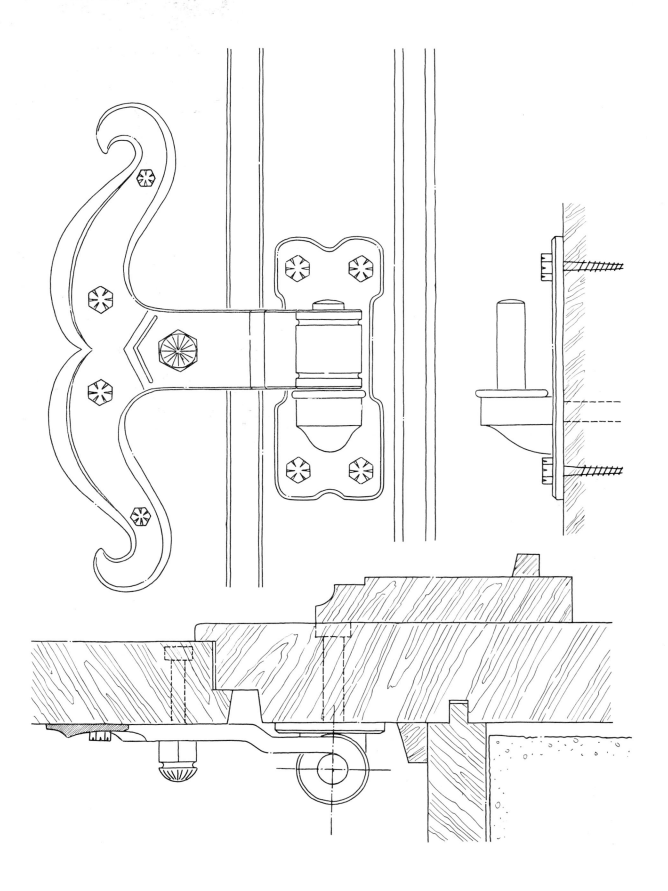

Left-hand page: Forged hinge for a wooden gate, working drawing.

Old double-panelled door on a Tirolean house.

Fifteenth century door with rich iron mouting, in the possession of the National Museum in Munich.

Wooden door covered with plates of sheet steel by means of hand-forged nails, surface red and other colours, lacquered, made for the Kyffhäuser Monument.

Right-hand page: Plates of sheet steel with various surface finishes screwed to a wooden door. Made for the Chapel of the Golden Madonna in the old cathedral church in Essen.

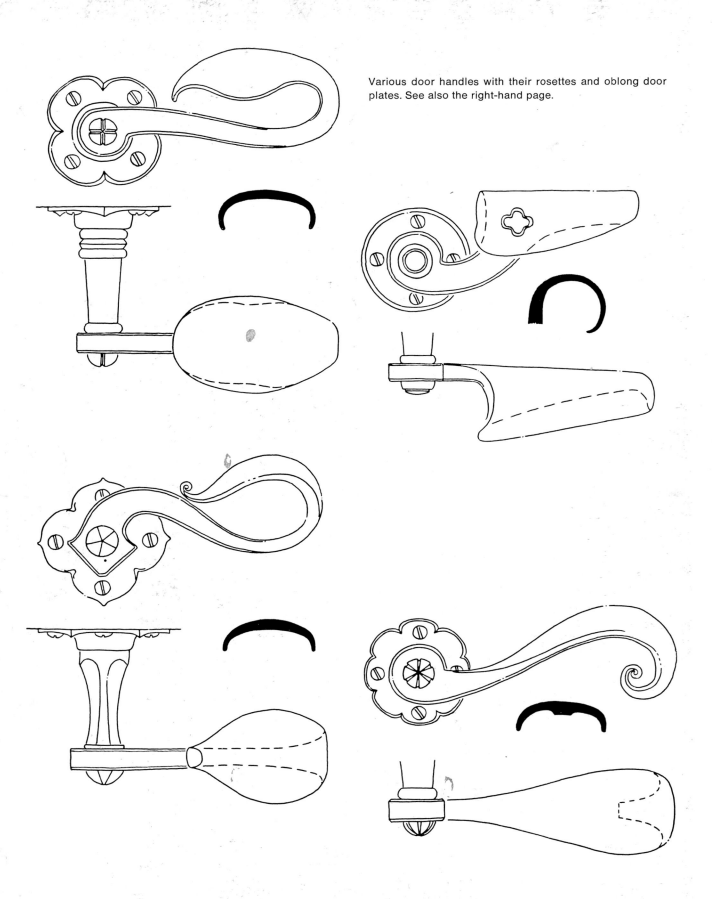

Various door handles with their rosettes and oblong door plates. See also the right-hand page.

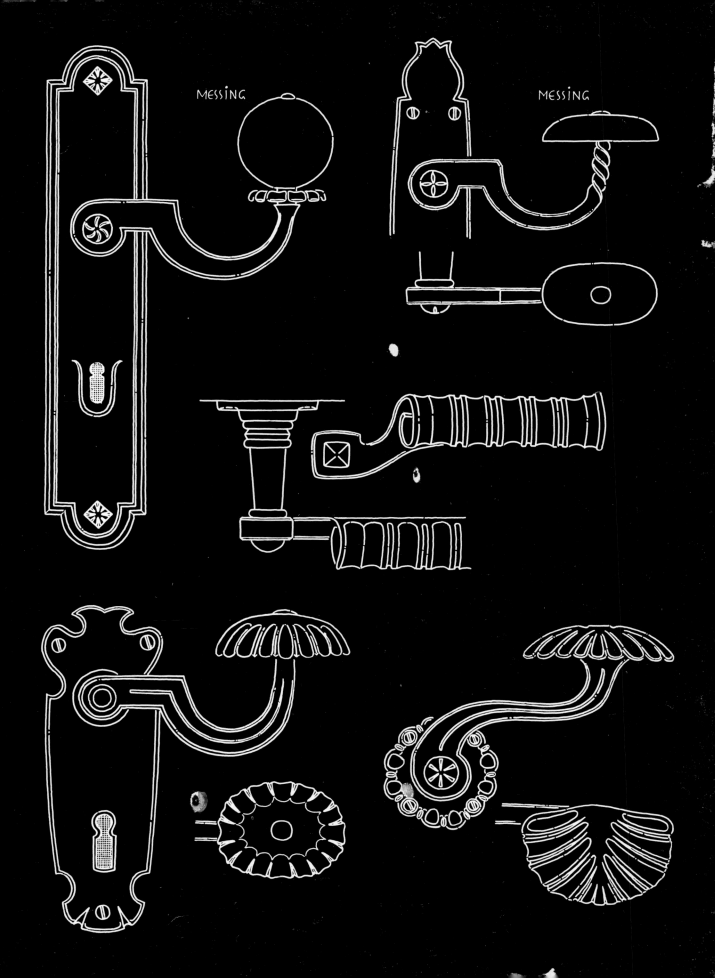

MESSING

MESSING

Book-ends forged from strong angle irons.

Right-hand page, top:
Book-end made from an angle of sheet metal, edge lightly hammered, both grooves and monogram chiselled, the ididivual petals of the rosette chiselled open and bent forward, black finish with gilding.

Gay ash-tray with candlestick, forged in iron.

Below: Raised aluminium ash-tray. The two cross bars for resting the cigarette on are copper.

My studio window. (The little "Bringer of Joy", forged in iron).

Sketch of a pen tray.

Letter-opener with "sea-horse" handle, forged in iron.

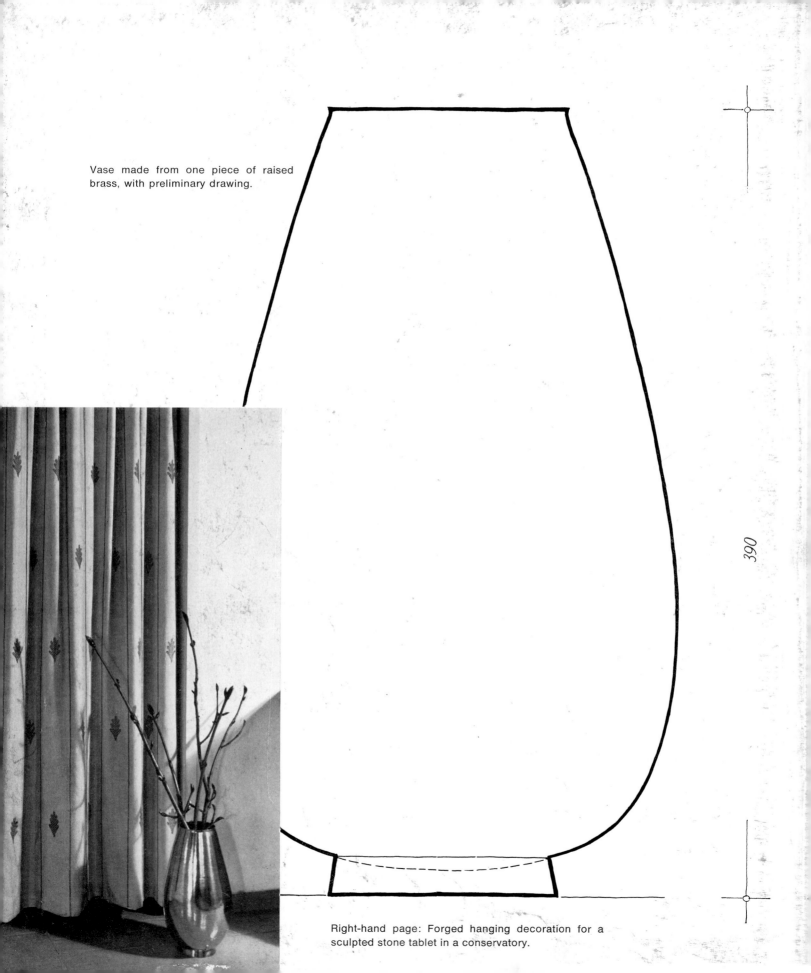

Vase made from one piece of raised
brass, with preliminary drawing.

Right-hand page: Forged hanging decoration for a
sculpted stone tablet in a conservatory.

PHOTOGRAPHS

Max Baur: p. 90 top. — Ursel Buchholz, Berlin: pp. 11, 15, 20 top and bottom, 21, 23 top and bottom, 24, 25, 28, 29, 30, 31, 35, 36 left, 40 top and bottom, 44 top, 45, 46, 48 bottom, 54, 55, 56, 57, 60 top and bottom, 61, 63, 64 top, 65 top, 70 top and bottom, 74 top and bottom, 75, 101 bottom, 109, 113, 114 middle, 116, 117, 120, 121, 138 top, 147 top right and bottom, 149. — Dewag, Berlin: p. 112. — Dipl.-Ing. A. Gebhardt: p. 81 top. — Helmut Körner, Dresden: pp. 22, 39, 118, 119. — Fritz Kühn, Berlin: pp. 13, 16, 17, 18, 26, 27, 32, 33, 37, 41, 42, 43, 44 bottom, 50 top, 52, 53, 64 bottom, 66, 67, 68, 69, 72, 73, 76, 77, 78 top, 79, 80, 81 bottom, 82, 83, 84 top and bottom, 85 top, 86 top, 87, 88, 89, 91, 92, 93, 95, 96, 98, 99, 101 top, 104, 106, 110, 111, 114 top left, 115, 124 top, 126, 127, 128, 129, 130, 131, 132, 134, 135, 137, 138 bottom, 139, 141, 142, 143, 146, 147 top left, 148, 150, 151. — Erich Rolle, Dresden: pp. 48 top, 49. — Alwin Seifert, Munich: p. 65 bottom. — Schweitzer-Brandenburg: pp. 50 bottom, 58. — Ernst E. Schwahn, Berlin: pp. 17 top, 85 bottom, 86 bottom. — Wienand Stockmann, Berlin: p. 36 right. — Harry Weber (Mauritius): p. 65 bottom.